KINGSTON AND WIMBLEDON TRAMWAYS

Robert J Harley

MP Middleton Press

Cover Picture: The sun shines on a trio of tramcars at
Wimbledon Broadway. On this June day in 1949 a tram
waits on the right of the picture for the space shortly
to be vacated by an Embankment bound car.
(J.H.Meredith)

Cover Colours: These are similar to the royal blue and
white livery applied to some trams in the original
London United Tramways fleet.

First published July 1995

ISBN 1 873793 56 1

© Middleton Press 1995

Design - Deborah Goodridge

Published by Middleton Press
            Easebourne Lane
            Midhurst
            West Sussex
            GU29 9AZ
            Tel: 01730 813169

Printed & bound by Biddles Ltd,
            Guildford and Kings Lynn

CONTENTS

GEOGRAPHICAL SETTING

Kingston and Wimbledon lie in a northern corner of the county of Surrey bounded by the River Thames. Before the establishment of Greater London in 1965, Hampton Court was situated in the county of Middlesex. North east of Wimbledon lies the area of the former London County Council. Although streets and houses now cover most of the area, several open spaces still exist such as Richmond Park, Wimbledon Common and the parkland surrounding the Palace of Hampton Court.

INTRODUCTION AND ACKNOWLEDGEMENT

The tramways featured in this book formed part of the large London United system which was conceived on a grand scale to serve the western and south western suburbs of the capital. This vision of supplying cheap and efficient public transport was promoted by the larger than life figure of Sir James Clifton Robinson, whose energy and enthusiasm for electric traction ensured that millions could benefit by the new transport services.

The story in pictures of the tramways of Wimbledon and Kingston has been made possible by the many photographers whose work appears in the following pages. My thanks go to C.Carter and John Meredith. I would particularly like to thank John Price and John Gent for all their help in locating suitable views. Rosy Thacker and Glynn Wilton at the library of the National Tramway Museum, Crich, Derbyshire, have supplied much rare material. No account of the former LUT lines would be complete without acknowledging the detailed reference works produced by Cyril Smeeton in 1995, and by Geoffrey Wilson in 1971, and also articles in various journals by the late R.E.Tustin. Tickets are from Godfrey Croughton's collection.

Finally I want to place on record my thanks to George Gundry of Wimbledon who has contributed photographs and personal memories, and has patiently answered all my enquiries. I trust this book will conjure up the sights and sounds of the golden age of London's tramways.

HISTORICAL BACKGROUND

Some settlements near the banks of the Thames date back to pre-Roman times. The conquerors from the south later created their own colonies joined by roads including Stane Street which connected London with Chichester and was in use by AD 70. After the departure of the Romans many centuries elapsed before the art of travel was further enhanced by the appearance of the London and Southampton Railway. Stations were opened in both Kingston and Wimbledon in 1838. However, the banks of the River Wandle had previously witnessed the inauguration of the world's first public railway, the Surrey Iron Railway, which connected Wandsworth with Croydon in 1803. This was essentially a horse drawn operation and the traffic of the SIR was later captured by the more modern steam railways.

The future leading light of the London United Tramways, James Clifton Robinson, was born in 1848. He had gained valuable experience in tramway operation on both sides of the Atlantic, before becoming Managing Director and Engineer of the LUT. He was knighted in 1905 and he had already shown the drive and determination needed to get his new transport system accepted by the travelling public and the powers that be. He possessed what later generations would describe as "charisma."

Kingston had to wait until the electric era to be equipped with tramways, when after protracted negotions, the LUT got a foothold in the town with the opening of lines on 1st March 1906. The initial routes were:

Hampton Wick - Kingston Bridge - Clarence Street.

Kingston Hill (George and Dragon) - Kingston (Eden Street) - Surbiton Station - Dittons (Winter's Bridge)

Surbiton Station - Tolworth (Red Lion)

Three years previously in April 1903, the sections between Twickenham and Hampton Court via Hampton Hill and Hampton Wick had opened for traffic. Further lines in the Kingston area followed in May 1906:

Kingston (Eden Street) - Richmond Road - Ham Boundary

Kings Road - Richmond Park (Kingston Gate)

Norbiton Church - Malden (Fountain)

The services operated were:

Richmond Bridge to Dittons
Malden to Hampton Court
Ham Boundary to Tolworth
Richmond Park Gates to Tolworth

Cars normally ran every ten minutes during the day on the above mentioned services.

The construction of the local tramways had involved much expense especially in connec-

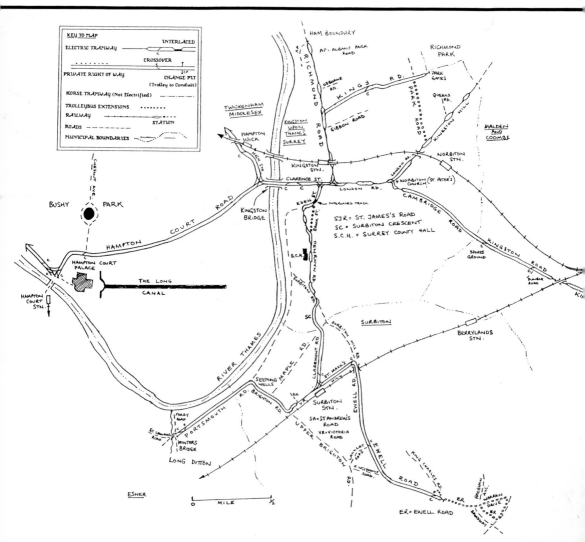

tion with street widening and the demolition of old properties in order to accommodate double track. Further works proceeded and Raynes Park Station was reached from Malden in April 1907. Raynes Park to Wimbledon via Worple Road followed the next month, with the Wimbledon Hill to Tooting, and Merton to Summerstown sections opening in June 1907. In October of the same year the LCC tramways were extended to meet the LUT lines at Longley Road, Tooting, but the metals were not connected. At that time through running was not contemplated, one factor in this decision was that LCC cars were equipped to run on the underground conduit method of current collection. LUT trams used the more conventional overhead trolley method.

Many of the LUT's planned extensions were to remain on the drawing board, and thus

In 1912 the LUT and the other tramway operator in Middlesex, the Metropolitan Electric Tramways, were absorbed into the London and Suburban Traction Company; the two companies' tram services were subsequently given numbers. The services operating in the Kingston and Wimbledon area were:

67 Hampton Court to Hammersmith
69 Richmond Bridge to Kingston
71 Tooting to Hampton Court
73 Dittons to Kingston Hill

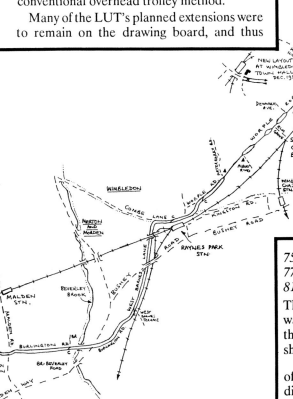

75 Ham Boundary to Kings Road
77 Tolworth to Richmond Park Gates
81 Merton (Haydons Road) to Summerstown

The Ham Boundary to Kings Road shuttle car was withdrawn in May 1920, and service was then restricted to occasional trips at factory shift times.

During the First World War maintenance of track and rolling stock became increasingly difficult, but with the return of peace a new realism began to sweep across the tramway operators in London. The tracks of the LCC and LUT were eventually joined at Tooting in May 1922 and a conduit/overhead wire change pit was installed. LCC services 2 and 4 were extended to Wimbledon Hill. The Merton to Summerstown shuttle service 81 continued to be operated by LUT cars from Fulwell Depot, whilst the Tooting to Hampton Court service 71 was cut short to terminate at the St.George's Road, Francis Grove loop in Wimbledon. In

potentially useful connections from Dittons to Hampton Court and from Kingston northward to Richmond and Barnes were never completed. This unsatisfactory situation had its effect on passenger numbers as competing motor buses were not inhibited by artificial traffic boundaries. Several LUT lines around Kingston never achieved a profitable existence and they became early candidates for service reductions and subsequent abandonment.

May 1926 LCC cars started a popular summer tradition of running over company lines all the way to Hampton Court, giving passengers a through journey from central London on services 2 and 4. However, the performance of the faster and more comfortable LCC trams rather showed up their LUT sisters, which increasingly became to be seen by the travelling public as antiquated and slow. Further erosion of the LUT's hold on the area occurred in April 1931 when LCC service 14 was extended along Plough Lane and Haydons Road into Wimbledon as a replacement of the former LUT service 81. However, by this time the wholesale conversion of the Kingston to Wimbledon tramways had been decided, with the trolleybus as the favoured replacement. In June 1931 trolleybuses started to operate between Twickenham and the new Kingston Hill loop replacing tram service 69. Other local conversions followed quickly and in September the newer vehicles began to substitute for tramcars on service 71 to Wimbledon. In December 1932 the Wimbledon tram terminus was cut back to outside the Town Hall, and the trolleybus wires were extended to form a terminal loop at the same location.

On the formation of the London Passenger Transport Board in July 1933 local services were as follows:

Trams

2/4 Wimbledon to Victoria Embankment
14 Wimbledon to Hop Exchange (London Bridge)

Trolleybuses

1 Twickenham to Tolworth, Red Lion
2 Dittons to Kingston Hill Loop
3 Tolworth to Kingston Hill Loop
4 Hampton Court to Wimbledon

These LT trolleybus routes were later renumbered in a series from 601 to 604.

The new board rapidly made it clear that it favoured the removal of tramcars from London's streets and one of the first fruits of this policy was the abandonment of the service 14 tracks in Haydons Road and Plough Lane in May 1934. Motor buses were used as a replacement. Elsewhere in the capital the tramway system was shrinking under the onslaught of the trolleybus, and Hampton Court lost its last tramway connection to London when service 67 was replaced by trolleybus 667 in 1935. The same fate awaited all of the former LCC services south of the river. However, the abandonment programme was halted in 1940 as a consequence of the Second World War and it was not until 1950 that sufficient motor buses became available to effect the extinction of London's tramways. The axe fell on Wimbledon on the night of 6th/7th January 1951 when services 2 and 4 were replaced by the 155 bus. The well known all night tram service from Tooting to central London also perished at the same time.

After the passing of the trams, conditions on the roads deteriorated throughout the 1950s and 1960s, when the private car, traffic congestion and lack of parking spaces all contributed to the situation which we all know only too well. The final nail in the coffin of pollution free electric traction came in May 1962 with the departure of the last trolleybus from Wimbledon to Kingston.

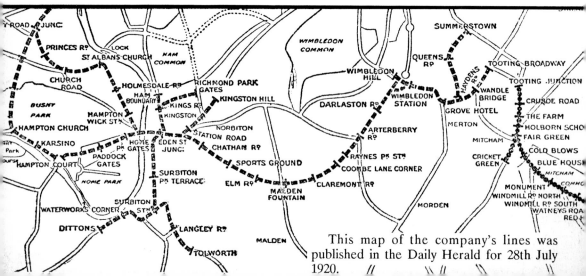

This map of the company's lines was published in the Daily Herald for 28th July 1920.

Tooting (Longley Road) to Merton (High Street)

1. Our tramway odyssey over the tracks of the capital has brought us to the meeting point of two systems. In the background the covered top LCC cars are disembarking passengers, some of whom have travelled from central London. Nearer to the camera stand LUT cars 296 and 168, the latter already fully loaded with its trolley pole turned in anticipation of immediate departure. (J.H.Price Coll.)

2. We pull back a little to observe two LCC cars on service 2 passing opposite the entrance to Longley Road, Tooting. Note the signs erected by the LUT which point potential passengers to the neighbouring South Metropolitan Tramways Co. terminus at Tooting Junction. This location is described in companion Middleton Press album *Croydon's Tramways*. (G.L.Gundry Coll.)

3. Car 263 dates from 1902 and belongs to a batch of trams which were originally turned out in royal blue and white livery. Many LUT cars later received top covers and from around 1909 onwards the standard LUT red and white livery began to replace the earlier colours. (J.H.Price Coll.)

4. A change pit was built to enable trams to alter their method of current collection at Longley Road, Tooting. This facility also allowed through working from the former LUT lines into the county of London where the LCC had constructed tramways which took power from an underground conduit. The gentleman walking towards the camera is carrying the plough fork which was used to guide conduit ploughs under trams proceeding north to Tooting and Clapham. Car 1849, on the right of the picture, already has its trolley on the overhead wire and it will shortly move forward to expel its plough where the centre conduit rail crosses the running rail in the foreground. (H.B.Priestley)

5. A plough is about to be forked under a tram
at the change pit. Note the details of the trucks
and the magnetic track brakes. (W.J.Haynes)

6. Another view of the change pit in operation
shows car 1813 outbound to Wimbledon. The
two gas lamps in the middle of the road helped
illuminate the scene at night and also penetrated the gloom of the winter fogs which
plagued London in the tramway era.
(W.A.Camwell)

7. Car 1839, in London Transport red and cream livery, ascends the grade to the railway bridge over the Tooting to Wimbledon line. The date is 29th May 1950. (J.H.Meredith)

8. At the start of High Street, Colliers Wood, we observe car 1841 about to cross the county boundary from Surrey into London. This administrative frontier was altered in April 1904 to run along the northern side of the railway. The poster which exhorts us to "Have a Capstan" is typical of a period when cigarette advertising was not subject to government health warnings. (D.A.Thompson)

9. Charringtons, the brewers, seemed to have purloined the traction standard to the right of car 1571 in this June 1949 view. This was an unusual arrangement and the use of the tramway pole to support the pub sign must date back to an earlier agreement made by the LUT. Those readers interested in buses might like to note STL 1759 on a Whit Monday 712 Green Line relief duty. (J.H.Meredith)

10. The bridge over the River Wandle in Merton was strengthened to receive the new LUT tramcars, one of which is pictured here not long after the opening of the service in June 1907. (J.H.Price Coll.)

11. A dismal scene in January 1951 is enacted by car 1829 on the last day of trams in Merton High Street. Remains of a more colourful past are to be found nearby, where Merton Abbey once stood. It was founded in 1117 and gave an education to Thomas a Becket, later to become the martyred Archbishop of Canterbury. (J.H.Meredith)

12. High Street, Merton is depicted in LUT days before the link up with the LCC in May 1922. Car 242 displays the service number 71 underneath the destination indicator. Even in those far off times motor traffic is beginning to compete for road space and the lady boarding the tram has to watch her step. (R.J.Harley Coll.)

13. Looking in the other direction to the previous picture, we catch sight of the High Street as it appeared in the first decade of the twentieth century. In this view the tramcar offers the only motorised form of road transport. (J.H.Price Coll.)

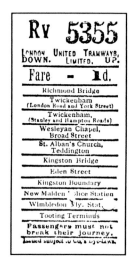

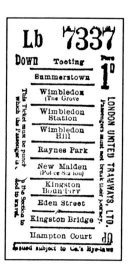

14. The shops are shuttered for the Bank Holiday as car 1798 is about to clatter over the crossover by Nelson Road. Unfortunately when this photo was taken in 1949 the crowds that once thronged the tramcars for a day out at Hampton Court were a thing of the past. (J.H.Meredith)

15. Just before the turn into Merton Road, car
1795 pauses at the traffic lights.
(V.E.Burrows)

No. 270.—CURTAILMENT OF SERVICE No. 14.

NOTICE TO INSPECTORS AND CONDUCTORS—WANDSWORTH, HAMMERSMITH, CLAPHAM AND THORNTON HEATH DEPOTS.

Commencing on Wednesday, 16th May, 1934, Service No. 14 will be curtailed to operate between Hop Exchange and High Street, Wandsworth, with workman journeys extended to Wimbledon Road (Garratt Lane). No tramway service will operate between Wimbledon Road (Garratt Lane) and High Street, Merton (via Haydon's Road), and the following transfer fares will in consequence be withdrawn :—

(i.) **5d.** and **6d.** ordinary transfer returns to and from—

(a) Trinity Road (Merton Road)
(b) High Street, Merton (Haydon's Road)   Change at High Street, Wandsworth.
(c) Queens Road (Haydon's Road)
(d) " Plough," Summerstown

(ii.) All maximum value transfer fares to and from Wimbledon via Haydon's Road. The transfers to and from Wimbledon via Clapham and Tooting will, of course, still be obtainable.

Additional 2d. Workman Transfers—Service Nos. 2, 4, 12 and 30.

To provide for passengers deprived of a direct service the following 2d. workman transfer fares will be instituted :
Trinity Road (Merton Road)—Wimbledon Road (Garratt Lane).
Haydon's Road (High Street, Merton)—Earlsfield Station.

Withdrawal of Service Nos. 12, 14, 26, 28 " B " Tickets.

The transfer journeys between Garratt Lane and Tooting and points along the Wandsworth Road will be provided for on the 5d. and 6d. ordinary return tickets, and in consequence the Service Nos. 12, 14, 26, 28, 5d. and 6d. " B " tickets will no longer be necessary and will be withdrawn from service.

Re-arrangement of Sections on Service Nos. 12, 14, 26, 28, 32, 89 Tickets.

Special attention is called to the re-arrangement of the order of sections on the 12, 14, 26, 28, 32, 89 ordinary single and 2d. workman tickets.

Side Destination Boards.

Revised side destination boards will be put into service with provision for cheap mid-day fares on the main board.

Specimens.

Specimens of the revised tickets and fare bill will be exhibited in the depots concerned.

Haydons Road and Plough Lane

16. Car 48, one of the oldest in the LUT fleet, is working the shuttle service 81T from Haydons Road Junction (with High Street, Merton) to Summerstown, where the lines met the tracks of the LCC leading to Garratt Lane. The suffix T was used in the 1920s to denote tram services operated by the LUT and MET companies. From May 1922 until LCC service 14 was extended in April 1931, this LUT line was isolated from the rest of the company system. Cars had to travel some distance from Fulwell to take up service. (R.Elliott)

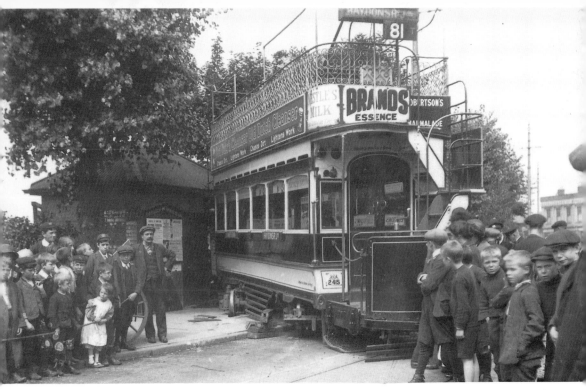

17. A slight contretemps outside the Recreation Ground in Haydons Road has become the centre of local interest as attempts are made to rerail this LUT car. The tramway company tried in November 1905 to purchase a site for a new depot near to the Recreation Ground. (G.L.Gundry Coll.)

18. Car 153 is not far from Haydons Road Station in this view dating from before the First World War. This stretch of road was the scene of an early LUT trolleybus experiment in 1922/23 when an AEC single decker underwent trials. Sadly this vehicle was the cause of a fatal accident when it collided with a cyclist at Plough Lane corner. The negative overhead wires erected for the trolleybus were removed in 1924, thus concluding for a while this pioneering LUT trackless venture. (J.B.Gent Coll.)

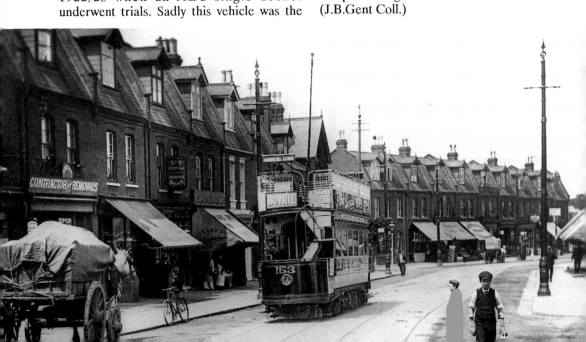

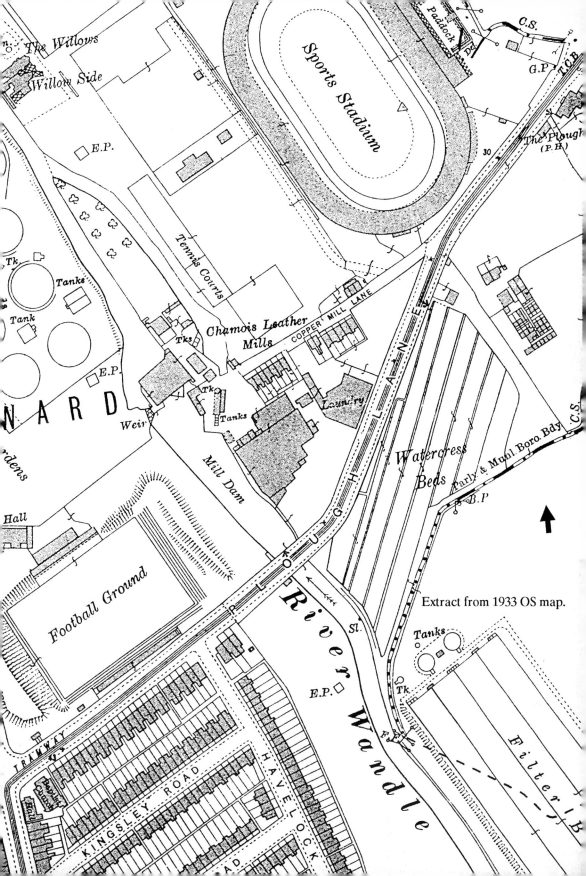

Extract from 1933 OS map.

19. We follow the tracks round into Plough Lane as car 180 heads for the terminus outside the Plough public house at Summerstown. Traffic on this route improved markedly with the opening of the Wimbledon Stadium in 1928. Extra trams were drafted in from Fulwell to cater for the passengers attending evening meetings at the stadium and the LUT would send a group of three rather elderly trams with a conductor acting as guard on the rear platform of the last vehicle. It was a favourite, if highly unofficial, sport of LCC motormen to bring their charges right up to almost the fender of the last LUT car in the convoy, in order to demonstrate the superior power and braking ability of the more modern LCC vehicle! Needless to say the poor LUT conductor probably breathed a sign of relief when the three older trams turned from Merton High Street to escape this LCC harassment. (R.J.Harley Coll.)

20. This tramcar obviously featured on someone's Christmas card for 1911! Underneath the superimposed seasonal message there lurks car 177 displaying two destination boards for the same location. (G.L.Gundry Coll.)

Merton Road to Wimbledon Hill

21. A tram on the Wimbledon Hill to Summerstown service eases its way round the corner of Merton Road and High Street. Across the road to the right of the tram is the future location of South Wimbledon tube station on the Northern Line which opened in 1926. (R.J.Harley Coll.)

D	0608	

**LONDON UNITED EL   :0 TRAMWAYS & HAMMERSMITH,
PICCADILLY, KING'S CROSS, FINSBURY PARK
TUBE RLY. (G. N., P. & B. RY.) & DISTRICT RAILWAY.**

THROUGH TICKET.
Via Hounslow Town or Hammersmith Broadway.

Change at Hammersmith	Hounslow Heath	4d
	Isleworth (Pears' Fountain)	3d
	Brentford	2d
	Turnham Green	1d

Change at Hounslow Tn

HAMMERSMITH

H. P. K.X. F.P. Tube Rly.	TO	Dist. Rly.
		THIRD CLASS ONLY.

on's Court Earl's Court	1d	Baron's Court West Kensington Earl's Court
Gloucester Road S. Kensington Brompton Road Knightsbridge Hyde Park Corner Downe Street Dover Street Piccadilly Circus Leicester Square Covent Garden Holborn	2d	High St., Kensing't'n Gloucester Road S. Kensington Sloane Square Victoria St. James's Westminster Charing Cross Temple
Russell Square King's Cross	3d	Blackfriars Mansion House Cannon Street Monument Mark Lane Aldgate St. Mary's Whitechapel
York Road Caledonian Road Holloway Gillespie Road Finsbury Park	4d	

22. This is the scene looking north along Merton Road. The tram on its way to Kingston and Hampton Court bears a poster urging horse racing enthusiasts to use the trams for their next visit to Sandown Park. (J.B.Gent Coll.)

.Extract from 1913 OS map.

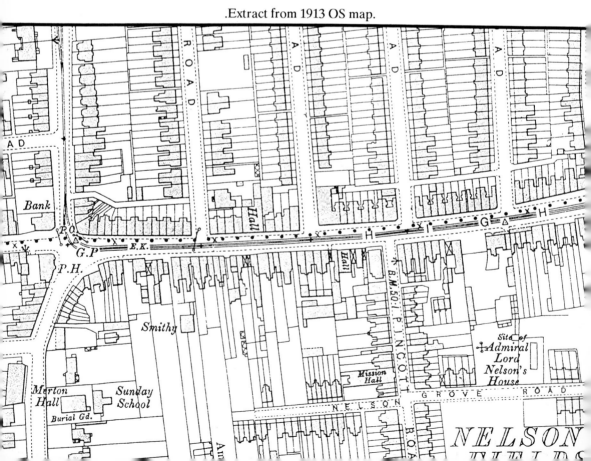

23. The bus behind car 1797 pauses opposite the start of one of the single track sections in Merton Road. The vast majority of the post war London system was double track. The single and loop arrangement shown here became a favourite with students of tramway trackwork. (J.H.Meredith)

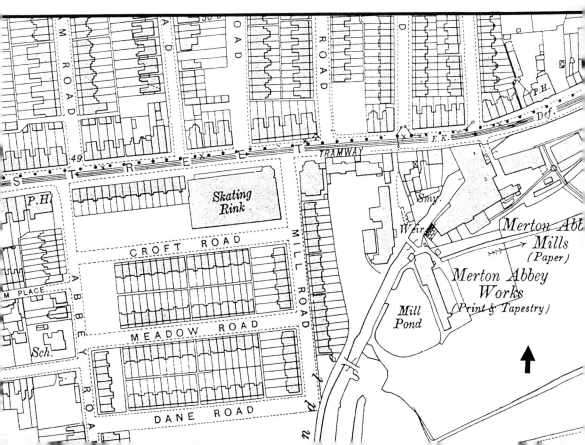

24. Obviously there wasn't much traffic at the corner of Merton Road when the intrepid photographer stood between the rails to record this view facing south towards the tube station. (A.J.Watkins Coll.)

25. A tram joins the single track by the entrance to Balfour Road; this first section of single line lasted a couple of hundred yards until the loop in Merton Road. (D.A.Thompson)

26. Opposite Pelham Road car 1797 swings into the loop. The signal on the traction pole to the left of the tram indicates with two horizontal lights that the following single track is occupied. The trolley of car 1797 will shortly pass under the skate in the overhead which will relay information to the signal to present "line clear" in the form of two diagonal lights. (J.H.Meredith)

27. On the other side of the road to the previous picture, we get another look at the signal in action as car 1795 passes the local branch of the Peoples Dispensary for Sick Animals. (C.G.Stevens)

28. An LCC car on service 14 slows in response to the red warning flags and the open trackwork repairs in Merton Road. (G.N.Southerden)

Automatic Signals—
Latimer Road, Merton

On and after 3rd January, 1940, signals will be fitted at the single track at Latimer Road, Merton, operated in the same way as those at The Grove, by contactor switches on the trolley wire. The signals mark the beginning and end of the signal section.

(1) **A GREEN** light at entrance to a section shews that it is unoccupied.

(2) **A WHITE** light indicates that a car is already in the section and proceeding ahead.

(3) **A RED** light indicates that a car is in the section and is approaching.

(4) **NO LIGHT** shewing indicates that the signals are out of order.

DRIVERS MUST NOT PASS UNDER THE CONTACTOR AT THE ENTRANCE TO THE SECTION UNLESS A GREEN LIGHT IS SHEWING.

The **DRIVER** passing under the contactor should see that the **WHITE** light appears, as this indicates that the signal has operated correctly and that the **RED** light is shewing at the opposite end ; he must watch the signal closely up to the last moment that the lights are visible and pass **SLOWLY** under the contactor.

The **CONDUCTOR** on leaving the section, must observe the clearing signal and in the event of its failing to change from **RED** to **GREEN**, inform his Driver who will warn the Driver of the first approaching car and the nearest Inspector that the signal has failed to clear.

In foggy weather when the lights are not visible, or when the signal is out of order, the Conductor must walk ahead and pilot the Driver past the signal.

Defective signals must be reported at once to the nearest Traffic Official.

29. Car 195 is seen on the short lived Wimbledon Hill to Summerstown service before it was curtailed to operate from Merton High Street. The road was then left free for the more important Tooting to Hampton Court link. However, transfer fares were made available for passengers wishing to use the Summerstown shuttle. (R.J.Harley Coll.)

LT Circular 2404

30. On the corner of Merton Road and The Broadway a tram halts as the motorman waits for the signal to proceed. (J.H.Meredith)

31. A relic from the past is this green and white LUT tram stop which was photographed in 1947 well into the London Transport era. (G.F.Ashwell)

32. The western end of Merton Road is nowadays part of Wimbledon Broadway. One of the burdens the LUT had to bear was its obligation to Wimbledon Council to supply expensive wood block paving across the whole width of the highway outside churches, schools and other public buildings. Thus the tramway paid for the very space that would be gleefully used by competing buses! (R.J.Harley Coll.)

33. The attraction of the latest form of electric traction is very apparent when comparing car 160 with its horse drawn rival. Meanwhile, the cyclist in the straw hat pedals past quite unconcerned. (J.B.Gent Coll.)

34. Car 291, pictured here approaching along The Broadway, was rebuilt with a top cover in 1910/11. This made better economic sense for tramway operators since an open top deck in inclement weather was not guaranteed to attract many passengers. Although these covers were an improvement when this view was published, later on in the 1920s the bodywork of these tramcars deteriorated and the upper saloon, such as it was, became a miserable, cold and draughty place to sit in the winter months. (J.B.Gent Coll.)

35. On 15th December 1932 the tramway between Wimbledon Hill and the Town Hall was abandoned and a new scissors crossover was installed for London bound trams to terminate outside the civic offices. (H.B.Priestley)

36. The lone tramcar in this picture is flanked by two trolleybuses from the first LUT series of tramway replacement vehicles. These particular trolleybuses were known in the transport world as "Diddlers" and appropriately number 1 survived to be preserved by LT. Its last outing under London wires was to close the system in May 1962. (K.H.Rudolph)

37. The shine on the rails indicates a well used scissors crossover. Car 1885 is on a Southern Counties Touring Society special in May 1948. As the London system contracted, the operation of private trams, hired by various transport clubs, increased and as the accompanying letter proves, London Transport seemed only too pleased to garner the extra revenue. (G.L.Gundry Coll.)

ROUTES 2/4	Wimbledon - Tooting - Clapham - Savoy Street	P.M. times are in heavy figures

Via Wimbledon Broadway, Merton Road, Merton High Street, Tooting High Street, Upper Tooting Road, Balham High Road, Clapham Common, Clapham High Street, Clapham Road, Route 2 via Kennington Road, Westminster Bridge, Victoria Embankment, return via Blackfriars Bridge, Blackfriars Road, London Road, Newington Butts, Kennington Park Road. Route 4 via Kennington Park Road, Newington Butts, London Road, Blackfriars Road, Blackfriars Bridge, Victoria Embankment, return via Westminster Bridge, Kennington Road

RAILWAY STATIONS SERVED : Wimbledon, South Wimbledon, Colliers Wood, Tooting Broadway, Trinity Road, Balham, Clapham South, Clapham Common, Clapham *SR*, Clapham North, Stockwell, Oval, Lambeth North, Westminster, Charing Cross, Temple, Blackfriars, Elephant & Castle, Kennington

Service interval : MONDAY to FRIDAY 4 minutes (evening 8-12 minutes), SATURDAY 4 minutes (evening 12 minutes), SUNDAY 5 minutes (evening 12 minutes)

	WEEKDAYS First				MONDAY to FRIDAY Last				SATURDAY Last					SUNDAY First				Last			
WIMBLEDON *Bdwy.*	....	....	....	4 54	5 48	9 9	9 15	10 15		9 21	9 33	10 15			....	....	7 41	8 24	9 0	9 15	10 15
Merton *Change Plt*	....	4 5	5 8	5 16	6 2	9 23	9 29	10 29	10 46	9 35	9 47	10 29	10 36		....	6 16	6 26	7 52	8 35	9 14	9 29	10 29	10 46
Tooting *Broadway*	....	4 6	4 32	5 9	5 17	6 3	9 24	9 30	10 30	10 47	9 36	9 48	10 30	10 37	11 21	4 7	....	6 17	6 27	7 53	8 36	9 15	9 30	10 30	10 47
Clapham Com. *Station*	4 15	4 19	4 45	5 25	5 33	6 19	9 40	9 46	10 46	11 3	9 52	10 4	10 46	10 53	11 37	4 23	4 57	6 33	6 43	8 6	8 49	9 31	9 46	10 46	11 3
Kennington Gate	4 25	4 29	4 55	5 37	5 45	6 31	9 52	9 58	....		10 4	10 16	....			4 33	5 9	6 45	6 55	8 16	8 59	9 43	9 58	....
Elephant & Castle	4 31	4 35	....	5 44	....		10 5	....			10 23	....			4 38		7 2	8 21			10 5	....
SAVOY ST. *Embkt.*	T4 43	T4 48	5 8	5 57	6 0	6 46	10 7	10 18		10 19	10 36	....		4 47	5 24	7 0	7 15	8 32	9 12	9 58	10 18

					*	†	†	†	*	†	†	†	*	*	†	†	†	*	†	†	†
SAVOY ST. *Embkt.*	....	....	T4 44	5 19	8 55	9 12	9 43	10 0	10 7	10 18	8 55	9 12	9 36	9 43	10 19	10 36	6 28	6 39	7 0	8 55	9 12	9 43	9 58	10 0	10 18
Elephant & Castle	....	....	4 57		9 8		9 56		10 20		9 8		9 56	10 32		6 41		7 13	9 8		9 56	10 11
Kennington Gate	....	....	5 4	5 30	9 15	9 27	10 3	10 15	10 27	10 33	9 15	9 27	9 51	10 3	10 39	10 51	6 48	6 54	7 20	9 15	9 27	10 3	10 18	10 15	10 33
Clapham Com. *Station*	3 46	4 21	5 16	5 42	9 27	9 39	10 15	10 27	10 39	10 45	9 27	9 39	10 3	10 15	10 51	11 3	7 0	7 6	7 32	9 27	9 39	10 15	10 30	10 27	10 45
Tooting *Broadway*	4 2	4 37	5 32	5 58	9 43	9 55	10 31	10 43	....	11 1	9 43	9 55	10 19	10 31	11 7	11 19	7 16	7 22	7 45	9 43	9 55	10 31	....	10 43	11 1
Merton *Change Pit*	4 3	4 38	5 33	5 59	9 44	9 56	10 32	10 44	....		9 44	9 56	10 20	10 32	....		7 17	7 23	7 46	9 44	9 56	10 32		10 44
WIMBLEDON *Bdwy.*	....	4 52	5 47	6 13	9 58	10 10					9 58	10 10					7 37	7 57	9 58	10 10	10 10

EARLY JOURNEYS—SUNDAY

Merton to John Carpenter Street at *5 29 a.m.
Merton to Savoy Street at †5 58 a.m.

Savoy Street to Merton at *4 48, *5 24, †5 39, *5 59 a.m.
John Carpenter Street to Merton at *6 15 a.m.
Clapham Common to Tooting *Broadway* at 3 49 a.m.

LATE JOURNEY—MONDAY to FRIDAY and SUNDAY

Tooting to Clapham Common at 11 3 p.m.

*–Via Blackfriars.   †–Via Westminster.   T–Time at Charing Cross.

LONDON TRANSPORT EXECUTIVE

Telephone
ABBEY 1234
Extension 85 or 202

Telegrams
PASSENGERS
SOWEST LONDON

55 BROADWAY
WESTMINSTER
LONDON, S.W.1

J. H. Price, Esq.,
Light Railway Transport League,
245 Cricklewood Broadway,
London, N.W.2.

20th February, 1952.

Ref. H61/PH

Dear Sir,

QUOTATION NUMBER 3177

I thank you for your enquiry of the 3rd February and have pleasure in quoting as follows. The charge for hiring   one tram   , constructed to carry   70 adult passengers, for the undermentioned journey on   Saturday 5th April, 1952 would be £3. 2s. 6d.   per vehicle   (subject to route approval)

Hirer to pay parking fees, if any.

Outward journey from   Highgate   departing at   –   via   direct route

Return journey from   tour, as attached   departing at   –   via   direct route
schedule Parts 1 and 2.

ALSO: 1 tram as per attached schedule (Part 1) £7. 5s. 0d.

This quotation is made subject to the vehicle or vehicles being available on acceptance thereof, and is based upon, and the vehicle or vehicles will be let subject to, the conditions printed on the back hereof.

If this quotation is accepted, please complete the appended form of acceptance and forward it to the Treasurer, London Transport Executive, together with the amount of the total hire charge or a deposit of 25 per cent. thereof. If 25 per cent. only of the total hire charge is paid at time of acceptance the balance is payable by the hirer 7 days before the date for execution of the order.

Cheques, money orders and postal orders should be made payable to the London Transport Executive and crossed "ACCOUNT PAYEE ONLY". Cash and notes should be sent only by registered post.

Yours faithfully,

62.

D. McKENNA

103/25 (1)
(10m 4.51-H61)

COMMERCIAL MANAGER

38. Cars 1531 and 1571 stand in the sunshine whilst a new Q1 trolleybus swings round behind on the start of its journey to Hampton Court. (H.B.Priestley)

39. A combination of road camber and well worn springs produces the effect of cars 1836 and 1802 leaning away from each other. The latter has also received external body bracing to see it through the twilight years until the one way journey to Charlton scrapyard. The streamlined vehicle glimpsed behind the trams is a Q1 class trolleybus. These outlived their railbound sisters only to be sold to a handful of Spanish operators in 1961. (C.Carter)

40. The trolley pole of the tram on the right is being swung in a marvellous evocation of period road transport. This picture captures the essence of a busy summer's day in the London suburbs around the year 1950. (D.Jones Coll.)

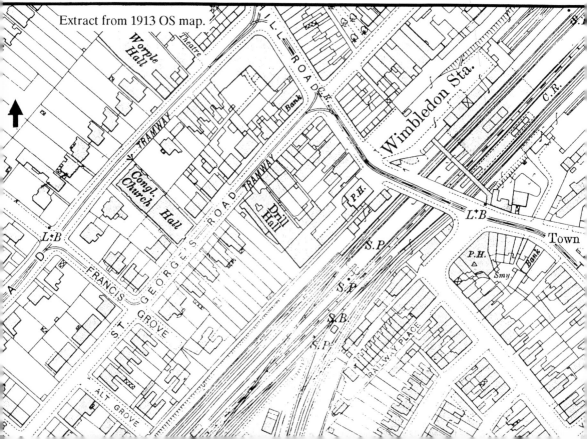

Extract from 1913 OS map.

41. In an era when walking in the middle of the highway did not invite instant annihilation, car 296 traverses the railway bridge by Wimbledon Station. The railways serving this area are described in the Middleton Press albums *Mitcham Junction Lines* and *Waterloo to Woking*. (J.B.Gent Coll.)

42. We now enter Wimbledon Hill Road in the company of LUT car 273; from the look of the crowd waiting to board it would seem to be "ladies first" on this car. (J.H.Price Coll.)

43. The rather primitive motor bus in this scene compares quite favourably with an equally antique LUT covered top car cresting the railway bridge. On a fine day like this nobody minded travelling outside on the top deck, and wholesome summer breezes could also be enjoyed whistling through the two window spaces in the centre of the tram's upper saloon. Note in the foreground the curve leading into St.George's Road. (J.H.Price Coll.)

44. On the left hand traction standard in Hill Road a sign is affixed giving details of the places served by the electric trams; to the right of the picture is a notice directing passengers to the nearby District Railway station. Electric trains first reached Wimbledon in August 1905. (J.B.Gent Coll.)

45. Car 291, which surfaced earlier in Wimbledon Broadway, now reappears as it is about to veer left into St.George's Road. (R.J.Harley Coll.)

46. Car 284 is negotiating the one way loop in St.George's Road. A trial car which ran here on 31st July 1906 to test the track alignment promptly derailed at the corner of Francis Grove. Matters were put right and a second run on 3rd August went without a hitch. The original tramway speed limit at this location was a stately eight miles an hour! (J.B.Gent Coll.)

47. In Hill Road by the Public Library car 160 heads east towards Summerstown. (J.H.Price Coll.)

48. The crew of this LCC bogie car take time to pose for the photographer in this view taken around 1930. This is the terminus in Wimbledon Hill Road and car 1849 will shortly depart on the 54 minute journey back to the Victoria Embankment. The return fare for a trip into London is eight old pence (4p), which rather puts into context the fantastic offer of "£5 A Week For Life" as advertised on the car dash. (Tramway Museum Society)

Wimbledon (Worple Road) to Malden

49. This postcard view of a brace of trams in Worple Road was sent in July 1907, a couple of months after the opening of these lines. The motorman of car 274 has a few words with the lady carrying the parasol, whilst his colleague on neighbouring car 272 swings the trolley. According to the indicator blind, one of these trams is poised for the rather long haul circling most of South West London to end up at Hammersmith. (J.H.Price Coll.)

50. Car 280 is one of the first arrivals at the new terminus and as such it has attracted the usual group of curious spectators, plus the obligatory policeman outside the Alexandra Hotel. (J.B.Gent Coll.)

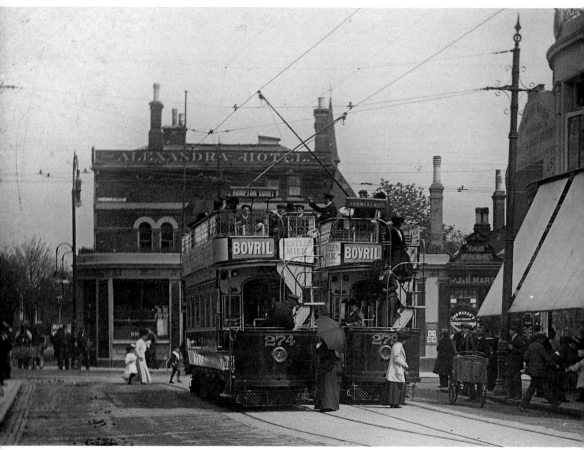

51. Gently does it, as the driver of car 1849 cautiously emerges from Francis Grove into Worple Road. Note the interlaced curve on the corner. LCC services 2 and 4 were extended to Hampton Court from 22nd May 1926, when through cars began operating on Saturday afternoons, Sundays and Bank Holidays. The 98 minute trip from the Embankment cost one shilling and fivepence (7p) return on Saturday afternoons and one shilling and elevenpence (9p) on Sundays. On its journey this tram crossed the Thames three times and traversed parts of four counties: Middlesex, Surrey, County of London and City of London. (D.W.K.Jones)

52. An LCC car heading north east along Worple Road, slows on its approach to the interlaced curve. (G.L.Gundry Coll.)

54. The church spire is in the background as LUT car 237 has just "looped" another sister LUT vehicle and an LCC car. The triangle an the dash contained the words EIGHT WHEEL BRAKES as a warning to motorists who came too close. (G.N.Southerden)

53. Car 269 nears the Methodist Church in Worple Road by Spencer Hill Road. This part of the route was constructed as single track and loops. (R.J.Harley Coll.)

WORPLE ROAD, WIMBLEDON

55. A view taken in the first decade of operation shows car 188 waiting to pass another tram. (R.J.Harley Coll.)

56. Car 262 is on the loop opposite Midmoor Road near what was then the grandstand of the celebrated All England Tennis Ground. The world famous international tennis event now takes place to the north of the town by Wimbledon Park. (J.H.Price Coll.)

57. At the corner of Arterberry Road a tramway signal protects the single track in Worple Road. No light showing would indicate track ahead clear. If the motorman saw a green light here, he could assume that a car already occupied the single track section ahead of him, but was heading in the same direction. A red light told the driver that a tram was approaching, and that he should not proceed. In the unlikely event of two trams reaching each end of the single line at the same moment, the London bound vehicle took precedence. (G.N.Southerden)

58. On the curve by Raynes Park Station the passengers on the top deck have a good view of the signal gantry on the London and South Western main line. Trams first reached this spot on 27th April 1907, some 69 years after the railway was opened. (G.L.Gundry Coll.)

59. In Coombe Lane near Durham Road car 287 now seems to be an accepted part of the scene and the horses do not appear to be at all perturbed by the electric cars. (R.J.Harley Coll.)

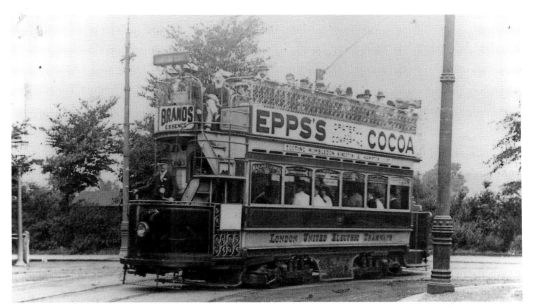

60. The rails now turn sharply southwards along West Barnes Lane. Notice that this car is equipped with a set of indicator boards and bears the full company title: LONDON UNITED ELECTRIC TRAMWAYS. In the first years of the company, great emphasis was placed on the word "electric", and rightly so, because the LUT had inaugurated London's first electric tramway on 4th April 1901. (J.H.Price Coll.)

61. West Barnes Lane was little more than a rural track before the arrival of the LUT. Here on the stretch near Raynes Park the passengers and crew of car 217 can still appreciate the bucolic surroundings before the great twentieth century suburban housing boom engulfs the place. (R.J.Harley Coll.)

62. Near West Barnes Farm we encounter a row of country cottages which would surely be dream abodes for the average tramway enthusiast. Imagine a sunny day like this one, with the sounds of the countryside mingling with the growl of an occasional passing tramcar. The striking royal blue livery of the tram would present a colourful spectacle, contrasting with the red brick and ivy covered walls of the cottages and the whitewashed fencing. (R.J.Harley Coll.)

63. A number of pictures were taken of the Board of Trade inspection of the section between Norbiton Church and Raynes Park Station. This momentous event occurred on 23rd May 1906. Car 321 contains LT. Col. Yorke, the government inspector, and Sir James Clifton Robinson, the LUTs Managing Director. The tram seems be coming to a halt in response to the policeman's raised arm; on the corner of Malden Road, an anxious mother grasps the hand of her offspring, who like all the other children, wants a closer look at the latest mechanical marvel. (R.J.Harley Coll.)

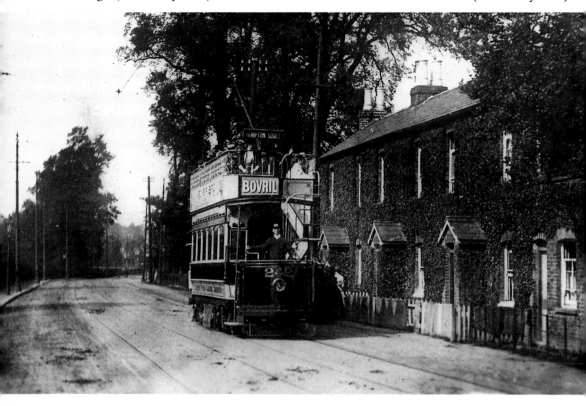

The delay in providing tram services prompted this rather sarcastic reponse from a Wimbledon postcard publisher.

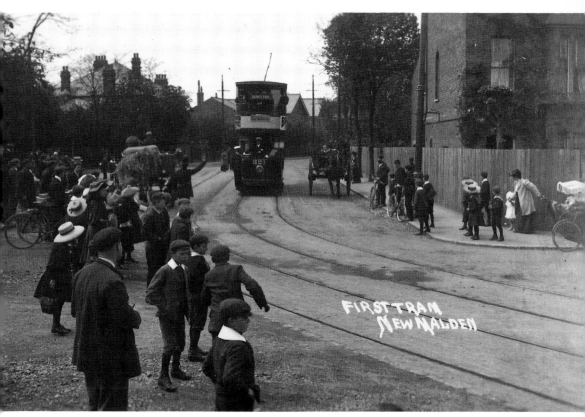

64. After the inauguration of a regular service to Malden, there was a delay until April 1907 before fare paying passengers were allowed to travel to Raynes Park. Here outside the Norbiton Park Hotel, also known as the Fountain, a car is seen on the Tooting to Hampton Court service. In the background the tracks and wires lead into Burlington Road. (R.J.Harley Coll.)

Wu 9936

DOWN	Fare	UP
Wimbledon Station	**1d**	Tooting
The Downs		Wandle Bridge
Raynes Park Stn.		Latimer Road
New Malden (Police Stn)		Wimbledon Station
Wellington Crescent		The Downs
Kingston Boundary		Raynes Park Stn.
Eden St. Junction		New Malden (Police Stn)
Home Park Gates		Wellington Crescent
Paddock Gates		Kingston Boundary
Hampton Court		Eden St. Junction

London United Tramways, Ltd.

Passengers must not break their journey. To which the passenger punched in the section to entitled to travel. Issued subject to Co.'s Bye-laws.

65. A temporary terminus was instituted at Malden and here we see car 310 about to reverse by using the crossover which is situated behind the photographer. This mostly nineteenth century urban development is often described as New Malden. (R.J.Harley Coll.)

66. In Kingston Road car 320 passes the Baptist Chapel at the corner of Westbury Road. (J.H.Price Coll.)

67. This 1907 view shows the Board Of Trade inspection car as it creeps carefully under the bridge carrying the London and South Western tracks to Kingston. Amongst the civil engineering works necessary for the passage of tramcars at this location, was the lowering of the roadway by 4ft. 6ins./1370mm and the consequent repositioning of four water mains and a sewer! (G.L.Gundry Coll.)

Kingston District

68. Car 236 has just traversed Cambridge Road and is now rounding the bend by St.Peter's Church, Norbiton. The lines straight ahead lead to Kingston Hill. (G.L.Gundry Coll.)

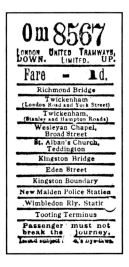

69. We now take a slight detour to investigate the Kingston Hill branch. Car 165 is about to pass Ye Olde Black Horse at the junction of Manorgate Road. Tram crews posted to this service were often treated to hot coffee and sandwiches supplied by Miss Janet Pearson. She also gave annual garden parties for the LUT staff. In an era when workers' rights were minimal, these acts of kindness were greatly appreciated. (J.B.Gent Coll.)

The LUT was alive to the power of advertising and in 1925 it commissioned F.Newbould to produce this poster extolling the charms of Kingston.

70. The rails ended by the George and Dragon, Kingston Hill. There was little housing development in this area and it is hardly surprising that this branch was one of the LUT's most unremunerative services. (G.L.Gundry Coll.)

71. Clarence Street, Kingston is one of the main commercial areas of the town. Although this picture looks dated, it is well to remind ourselves that for many cities in the world, the concept of trams running through pedestrianised shopping precincts, is a thoroughly practical one. Modern light rail vehicles enhance the quality of urban life and are pollution free. (J.B.Gent Coll.)

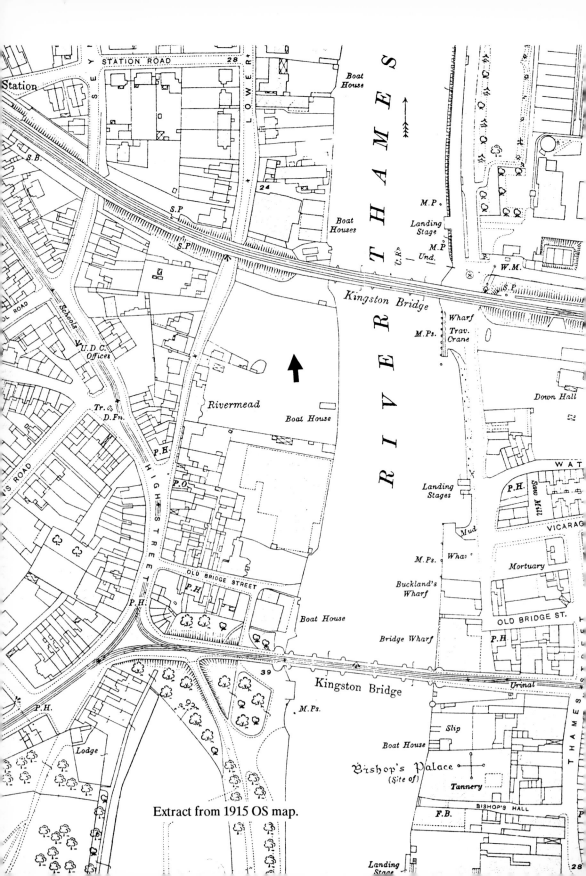

Extract from 1915 OS map.

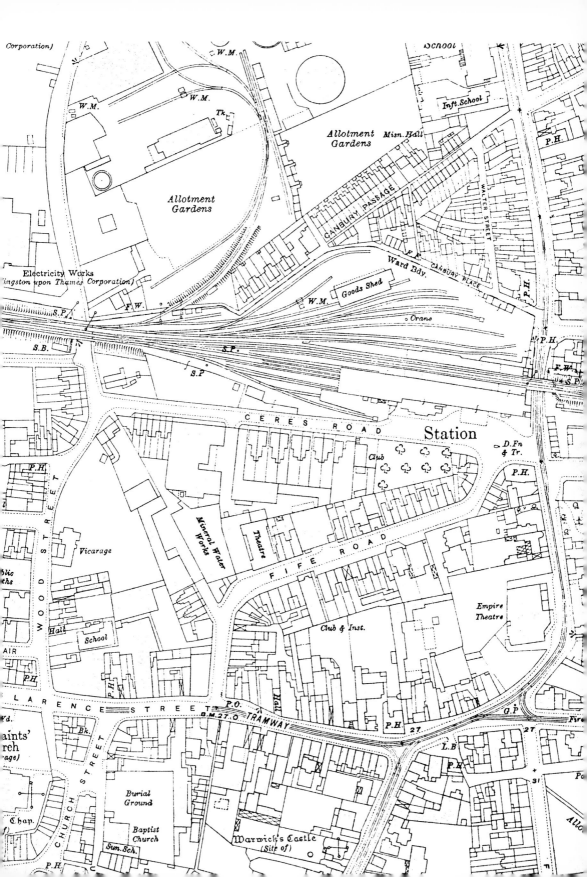

72. The days of the trams are numbered in this picture as the new trolleybus stop testifies. Car 297's working life is drawing to a close and by the end of 1931 trams would be a memory on the streets of Kingston. (G.L.Gundry Coll.)

73. Opposite the Crown and Thistle in Clarence Street a motorist tries a risky manoeuvre to overtake car 300 en route to Tooting. (Lens of Sutton)

74. A final look at Clarence Street reveals a 10 mph speed limit sign attached to the traction standard in the foreground. The town was once notorious for police speed traps and the local AA "scouts" often used to warn motorists by NOT saluting as they drove past. (G.L.Gundry Coll.)

75. We now journey south of the town centre along Claremont Road, Surbiton. Car 179, on the Dittons service, passes the clock tower at the junction of The Crescent. The stop signs are most informative; note that the Dittons terminus is referred to as Windows Bridge. (G.L.Gundry Coll.)

76. The tram in the distance by the clock tower is one of the T class covered top cars which inaugurated services in the Kingston area. Unfortunately for the locals these splendid vehicles were transferred to the Hounslow and Uxbridge Road routes in Middlesex from the spring of 1907. Therefore their sojourn on Surrey tracks lasted barely a year. Much grumbling resulted when these fine red and white liveried cars were replaced by the "standard" LUT open toppers.
(G.L.Gundry Coll.)

77. "Where are the snows of yesteryear?" This is often the lament of people more concerned with global warming than the practicalities of getting to work in winter in the 1990s. In the early years of this century, however, it was a matter of pride amongst tramway workers that the cars ran whatever the weather. On this cold and icy day at the junction of Claremont Road and Victoria Road, the idea of frozen points delaying the service would have been laughable to the hardy souls then operating the tramway. (G.L.Gundry Coll.)

78. Just across the way from Surbiton Station a couple of cyclists have time for a chat by the three way tramway junction of Victoria Road, Claremont Road and St.Mark's Hill. In the 1920s the east to west connecting tracks from St.Mark's Hill to Victoria Road were removed. They had been disused for many years. (G.L.Gundry Coll.)

79. At the same location as the previous photograph, only the presence of a type T "Palace" car fixes the year at 1906. From the look of the overhead and the state of the roadway, it would seem that the connecting tracks to St.Mark's Hill have yet to be installed. (G.L.Gundry Coll.)

80. Car 252 negotiates the points in Victoria Road before a straight single track section which left room for carriages and carts to park outside the shops. (R.J.Harley Coll.)

81. Where the Portsmouth and Brighton roads meet is known as Waterworks Corner. Here car 162 prepares to turn towards Surbiton. (G.L.Gundry Coll.)

82. When this route was first constructed, the terminus outside the Masons Arms, Long Ditton was regarded as purely temporary pending the completion of an extension via Thames Ditton and Esher to cross the Thames at Hampton Court. However, this useful link was never built. (G.L.Gundry Coll.)

83. According to some official sources the bridge over the stream by the tram terminus should be called Winters Bridge. The LUT referred to it as Windows Bridge on tram destination blinds. Whatever the fuss about names, the tram here provided a convenient, cheap and reliable means of transport for the local inhabitants. (J.B.Gent Coll.)

Extract from 1913 OS map.

84. Ewell (pronounced "yule") Road, Surbiton leads to the LUT terminus at Tolworth. This postcard view appeared in 1906. (J.H.Price Coll.)

85. Further along Ewell Road, an open top car is caught in time opposite the Prince of Wales. On the left of the tram the presence of the garage sign and the Castrol plaque indicate that the internal combustion age has firmly taken root. (G.L.Gundry Coll.)

86. Car 151 waits in the sunshine outside the Red Lion pub in Tolworth where the tramtracks ended. Service 77 was converted to trolleybuses in July 1931 and the wires were later extended to Tolworth, Warren Drive in September 1933, by which time London Transport was firmly in the driving seat. (G.L.Gundry Coll.)

RD KINGSTON

87. An earlier arrival at Tolworth terminus is car 327 freshly delivered and in sparkling condition with Venetian Red painted waist panels and dashes. Fleet numerals and side lettering were gold with blue shading. The coming of the trams finally ended the rural nature of Ewell Road where the famous naturalist and author, Richard Jeffries, lived in 1877-82. (C.Carter Coll.)

88. On Richmond Road the highway had to be lowered under the railway bridge to permit the operation of double deck tramcars. Again, all this work was paid for by the LUT. (G.L.Gundry Coll.)

89. These lines in Kings Road were built to serve the northern suburbs of Kingston. As can be seen, even the "back street" routes of the LUT were constructed to the highest standards with double track and span wire suspension. (G.L.Gundry Coll.)

90. In 1648 in the last major engagement of the Civil War, the armies of Parliament fought off an attack on Kingston by Royalists. The military theme continues with this view of the East Surrey Barracks in Kings Road. A member of the forces of the Crown is about to board car 225. (G.L.Gundry Coll.)

91. Christopher John Spencer became Manager of the LUT/MET combine in November 1918. He was interested in cutting costs on some of the weakest LUT lines, and in 1922 the one man operated tram, seen here at Richmond Park Gates, was placed in service. The novelty of the occasion is not lost on at least one potential passenger, who seems totally non-plussed as to the way into the car! (G.L.Gundry)

92. It is probable that the first Kingston Bridge was built by the Saxons, however, a structure at this location was recorded in 1219. The bridge illustrated here dates from 1828 and it was widened in 1914, during the tramway era. This prospect of Kingston from the bridge is a scene from a vanished world. It depicts a by-gone age of tramcars, horse drawn carts, Mazawattee Tea and Good Stabling at Ye Olde Row Barge. (G.L.Gundry Coll.)

94. "The Bystander" for 14th March 1906 contained this picture attached to a rather sour by-line complaining that the bridge was practically a tramway track, and that: "this state of affairs has aroused the most outspoken indignation in the neighbourhood." As usual the rich and privileged had to have their moan, but most fair minded folk were excited by the three car opening procession, with the leading tram driven by the Mayor of Kingston ably assisted by Sir James Clifton Robinson. (R.J.Harley Coll.)

93. "Opening Trams Kingston March 1 1906" is the inscription on this card which records the triumphal procession of the first tram. Flags and bunting adorn the bridge and many Kingston businesses closed for the day to welcome the electric age to the town. (G.L.Gundry Coll.)

95. We now take a position on the Middlesex
bank of the Thames, as we look out over this
post First World War scene. The criticisms of
"The Bystander" no longer have any relevance
as this lone tramcar glides through the vacant
road space. (G.L.Gundry Coll.)

**Other views of this location
are included in** *London to
Portsmouth Waterway* **album
(Middleton Press).**

96. This tram has obviously come to grief on the points at the Hampton Wick side of the bridge. Although a least one bogie has left the track, the trolley is still on the wire, which rather suggests that the postcard publisher was overdoing it with the "Tram Smash" headline. (J.B.Gent Coll.)

97. Before the use of automatic point controllers which operated on the power or coast principle, the LUT employed the device pictured here. A pointsman moved a lever in the pavement to switch the points and the pillar supporting coloured lamps revolved. A green or a white light then showed, depending on the route set by the pointsman. (R.J.Harley Coll.)

98. The Richmond Bridge to Windows Bridge(Long Ditton) service ran from 1906 to 1908, thus we can date this view fairly accurately. As one might expect from the LUT, this triangular junction was laid out on the grand scale with plenty of space for the electric cars and an island refuge for pedestrians. (J.H.Price Coll.)

99. On 2nd April 1903 the section of track opened between Stanley Road Junction and Hampton Court, via Hampton Wick; two days later the western half of the loop via Hampton Hill was put into operation. Car 212 is seen in Hampton Wick around 1904. (R.J.Harley Coll.)

100. A view of Hampton Wick High Street in
early tram days depicts car 231.
(R.J.Harley Coll.)

101. In order to get the LUT constructed,
James Clifton Robinson had to engage in a
battle royal with hostile local authorities and it
is calculated that at one time he was carrying
on negotiations with no less than 30 councils
and three county councils! He also had to put
up with the machinations of Sam Fay, the
LSWR's Traffic Superintendent, who used
every trick he could to prevent the tramways
taking traffic from the railway. Here at
Hampton Wick Station, car 222 passes under
the tracks of the rival operator. Another
picture, taken very near this spot, is included
in Middleton Press album *Kingston and
Hounslow Loops*. (C.Carter Coll.)

102. The road from Kingston Bridge to
Hampton Court offered a pleasant tram ride
where the motorman could afford to increase
the speed in anticipation of few stops until the
terminus was reached. At the Greyhound
Hotel car 216 stops to pick up a passenger.
(R.J.Harley Coll.)

103. Artistry of a high calibre can be admired in the Lion Gates, Hampton Court, which are attributed to Jean Tijou, a pupil of Sir Christopher Wren. The wrought iron tracery work on the tramcar is the product of unknown craftsmen employed by Geo.F.Milnes & Co. Ltd.. (G.L.Gundry Coll.)

104. Noon in the main street, Hampton Court, sees car 278 having passed the crossover outside the Queens Arms. The clutch of buildings served the needs of the many trippers who descended on the area in the summer months. Refreshments, both alcoholic and the afternoon tea variety, are on offer to travellers. (G.L.Gundry Coll.)

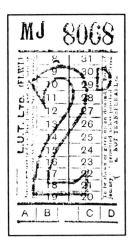

105. Looking in the other direction to the previous view, the mass of this 1928 Bank Holiday traffic is well up to modern standards. The General buses, the LCC tramcar and the wide variety of late 1920s touring and saloon cars, all add to the confusion. (LCC official view)

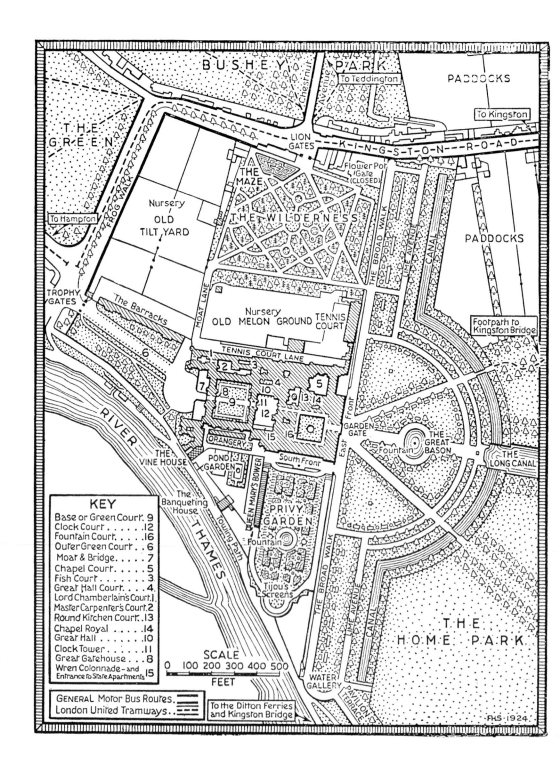

Hampton Court from the London's
Underground 1924 guide book.

106. Appropriately the Kings Arms Hotel faces the Queens Arms across the tramtracks. What a contrast between this view taken in the first decade of the century and the traffic jam in the previous picture. (G.L.Gundry Coll.)

107. We arrive finally at the end of the line. Here a tram is made ready for the return journey to Wimbledon. This terminus was not equipped with a trolley reverser so the whole thing had to be done manually. This demanded a steady hand and a keen eye to get the trolley on the wire first time. (G.L.Gundry)

108. This covered top car is depicted towards the end of its career. Notice that it has been fitted with magnetic track brakes. On the side of the tram, passengers are reminded of the through bookings available with the Underground. This arrangement made an excursion into town an attractive proposition. (G.N.Southerden)

→

109. The terminus at Hampton Court was featured on many postcards. Car 223 stands with its crew on the terminal stub for service 67 to Hammersmith via Twickenham and Brentford, whilst the tram opposite waits to depart in the direction of Kingston. (G.L.Gundry Coll.)

→

110. The Trophy Gate behind car 173 leads the the Outer Court of the Palace. The road on the right leads to Hampton Court Bridge and East Molesey. Unfortunately the LUT's expansion plans were thwarted in this direction, and the travelling public was deprived of another Thames crossing by tramcar. (C.Carter Coll.)

111. We end our tramway tour with this fine study
of LUT car 281 waiting to transport us back to
London, via Twickenham and Hammersmith.
(S.E.Letts Coll.)

Cars 301-340. These trams were ordered by the LUT for the opening of the Kingston lines in 1906. They were built at Preston by the United Electric Car Company. At the time of their delivery they were considered by many to be the finest trams ever to grace the streets of Great Britain, and as such they attracted considerable attention. A measure of this interest can be gauged by the extract from the ICS reference work on tramways published in 1908, and illustrated overleaf.

112. Car 303 is seen in original condition in 1906. Note the two indicator boards on the side of the car. These trams were known as "Palace" cars and were later classified type T. All of this batch were moved from the Kingston area to operate on the Hounslow and Uxbridge services. (Tramway Museum Society)

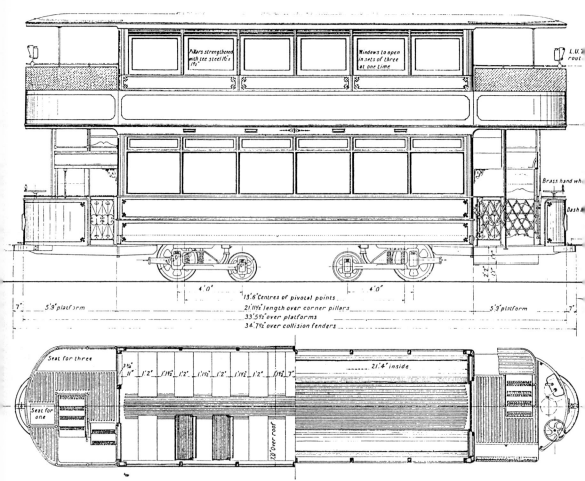

Deck Covered Bogie Car—London United Tramways.

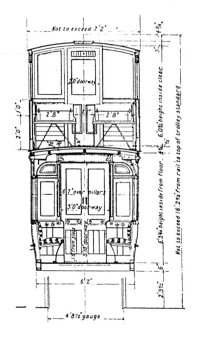

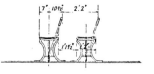

113. In 1925 this class was modernised with new traction motors, comfortable upholstered seats on both decks, new interior fittings and improved headlights. Car 312 is captured on film at Southall shortly after the LT takeover in 1933. (C.Carter)

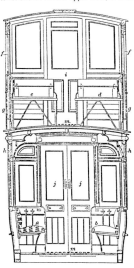

In the type of car illustrated, seating accommodation is provided for 74 passengers, 30 on the lower and 44 on the upper floor, or deck. The seats *a, b* on the lower floor are longitudinal, while those *c, d* on the upper are cross-seats with swing backs, so that passengers can face either the front or rear; in addition, four passengers can be accommodated at each end on the outside fixed seats *e.* On the older types of double-deck cars, the top seats were open and no protection from the weather was afforded to the passengers travelling on the outside of the car. The modern tendency is to build a roof over the top seats, and, by carrying the sides up to the roof, to enclose the top deck as well as the lower deck by means of panelling and windows. The upper windows *f* are in this case arranged to open, by lowering them into a space provided behind the top-deck panelling *g.* The small windows *h* of the lower deck can be opened for ventilation, but the main windows are fixed. Some-times, however, all the side windows of a car are arranged so that they can be thrown open in hot weather. Single sliding doors *i* are provided at the ends of the car on the upper deck, and double sliding doors *j* below. Stairways *k* are built to give access to the upper deck at both ends of the car. They are built as left- and right-handed spirals and, as in the present instance, in two straight portions, with a small intermediate platform *l* between them. The car floors and platforms are protected with wearing strips, or slats, *m* ; by renewing the slats from time to time, the solid floor is kept sound. The upper platforms are

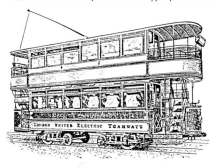

surrounded by metal screens *n,* and each lower platform can be closed by a swinging gate *o* and a collapsible gate *p.* When driving the car, the driver, or motorman, stands between the stairway and the dash *q,* where he has room to operate the brake hand wheel *r* and controller *s.* The total length of the car over the collision fenders is 34 feet 7½ inches, the maximum width 7 feet 2 inches, and the height 15 feet 10 inches.

114. This Type T car has been fitted with driver's windscreens and it is painted in the final LUT red and white livery with the London United fleet name on the waist panel. (Tramway Museum Society)

115. The demise of these fine trams was hastened by the trolleybus conversions of 1935-36. Here we see car 2352, renumbered by its new owners and sporting London Transport livery. (G.N.Southerden)

Car 341. This vehicle can truly be regarded as before its time. Reconstructed from damaged MET car 132, it was sent over to the LUT and put back on the road in 1922. It was a fully enclosed car equipped with front entrances, which facilitated one man operation with the motorman able to work an automatic ticket machine. The tram worked initially service 77, Richmond Park Gates to Tolworth, however, the experiment was only partly successful and it was later transferred to service 55, the Brentford to Hanwell shuttle. Here it was joined by three other converted eight wheelers, cars 342-344. Car 341's original 8ft. 6ins. single truck was later replaced by a pair of Brill 22E bogies. The experiment ended suddenly in 1928, when all the one man cars were withdrawn and service 55 reverted to conventional operation. It is believed that car 341 escaped the mass LUT scrappings of 1931 and spent its retirement years on an estate in East Molesey.

116. The ends of the advertising boards on car 341 have a fairground look about them as can be seen from this photo. However, the message was not a commercial one, but a plea for greater road safety. Aside from this, the tram was painted standard LUT red and white. Notices by the door read PLEASE HAVE EXACT FARE READY and PLEASE PAY AS YOU ENTER CAR. Note the roof mounted headlamps. (LUT official photo)

117. Inside car 341 could be found this handy "road guide", which in the absence of a cheerful conductor calling out the stops, was intended to give the precise location of the car. The device was linked to one axle of the tram and it also showed the route for one half mile ahead. As with many pioneering contraptions, this one couldn't stand the pace, and often it failed to keep up with the tram's progress or simply broke down and refused to budge. (LUT official photo)

118. Car 341 was initially shedded at Fulwell before its transfer to Hanwell for service 55. The other two trams in this picture are an LUT works car and one of the eight wheel one man operated cars. (G.L.Gundry Coll.)

Finale

119. The London County Council Tramways Trust will soon be starting work on their latest project, the full restoration of an LUT class W car as illustrated here. The cost of this restoration is estimated at £80-100,000 and the speed of progress depends very much on donations. If you would like to help by making a financial contribution, please contact: The Treasurer, LCCTT, 36 Cranley Drive, Ilford, Essex, IG2 6AH., from whom more details can be obtained. (C.F.Klapper)

Trolley Bus Service—Twickenham to Teddington

On Saturday, May 16th, the first of the new Trolley Buses, which are to replace Tramcars on some of the London United Tramway routes, will be put into service between Twickenham and Teddington Railway Station.

Simultaneously, the Tramcar service (Route 69) between these points will be withdrawn, and passengers travelling from Kingston to Twickenham, and vice versa, will transfer from Tram to Trolley Bus at Teddington. The vehicles will be timed to facilitate connections.

Transfer tickets will be issued, and these should be produced for inspection on the second stage of the journey.

The Trolley Bus Service will be extended to Kingston, and additional routes instituted to Tolworth, Wimbledon, and The Dittons as soon as further new vehicles are available.

York St., Twickenham
Twickenham Fountain
Stanley Rd. Junction   1d.

Princes Road
Church Rd., Teddington   2d.
  (TRANSFER TO TRAM)

St. Albans Church
Holmsdale Road   3d.

Hampton Wick Station
Eden Street, Kingston   4d.

FIRST & LAST TIMES

Weekdays	First	Last
Twickenham–Kingston	6.45	11.7
Kingston–Twickenham	6.21	11.7
Sundays	First	Last
Twickenham–Kingston	9.0	11.16
Kingston–Twickenham	9.0	11.7

120. The tram rails are derelict and a replacing trolleybus heads for Twickenham. The LUT trolleybus network formed the basis of the later LT system, which in its day was the largest in the world. An achievement which Sir James Clifton Robinson would have thought only right and proper. (LUT official photo)

MP **Middleton Press**

Easebourne Lane, Midhurst, West Sussex. GU29 9AZ
Tel: 01730 813169   Fax: 01730 812601

Tramway Classics

Brighton's Tramways

Camberwell & West Norwood Tramways

Croydon's Tramways

Dover's Tramways

East Ham & West Ham Tramways

Embankment & Waterloo Tramways

Exeter & Taunton Tramways

Greenwich & Dartford Tramways

Hastings Tramways

Lewisham & Catford Tramways

Maidstone & Chatham Tramways

North Kent Tramways

Southend-on-Sea Tramways

Southampton's Tramways

Southwark & Deptford Tramways

Thanet's Tramways

Victoria & Lambeth Tramways

Local Railway Albums

Clapham Junction to Beckenham Junction

East Croydon to Three Bridges

London Bridge to Addiscombe

London Bridge to East Croydon

Mitcham Junction Lines

South London Line

Victoria to East Croydon

West Croydon to Epsom

Waterloo to Windsor

Write or telephone for our full list of railway, local history, bus, military and waterways albums